MY NOTARY
JOURNAL

NOTARY INFORMATION	
Name :	
Address :	
Phone Number :	**Fax number :**
Email Address :	

LOG BOOK INFORMATION	
Log Book Number :	
Start Date :	**End Date :**

NOTARY RECORD

Full name :	Phone number :	Thumb print :
Email Address :	Signature :	
Address :	**Signer's Signature**	

Service Performed	Identification		ID Number :	
☐ Jurat	☐ ID Card	☐ Credible Witness		
☐ Oath	☐ Passport	☐ Known Personally	Issued by :	
☐ Acknowledgement	☐ Drivers License		Date Issued :	Expiration Date:
☐ Other :	☐ Other :			

Witness Full name :		Phone number :	
Email Address :		Witness Signature:	
Address :			
Document Type	Date/Time Notarized	Document Type	Fee Charged
			Record Number

NOTARY RECORD

Full name :	Phone number :	Thumb print :
Email Address :	Signature :	
Address :	**Signer's Signature**	

Service Performed	Identification		ID Number :	
☐ Jurat	☐ ID Card	☐ Credible Witness		
☐ Oath	☐ Passport	☐ Known Personally	Issued by :	
☐ Acknowledgement	☐ Drivers License		Date Issued :	Expiration Date:
☐ Other :	☐ Other :			

Witness Full name :		Phone number :	
Email Address :		Witness Signature:	
Address :			
Document Type	Date/Time Notarized	Document Type	Fee Charged
			Record Number

NOTES

NOTARY RECORD

Full name :	Phone number :	Thumb print :
Email Address :	Signature :	
Address :	Signer's Signature	

Service Performed	Identification		ID Number :	
☐ Jurat	☐ ID Card	☐ Credible Witness		
☐ Oath	☐ Passport	☐ Known Personally	Issued by :	
☐ Acknowledgement	☐ Drivers License		Date Issued :	Expiration Date:
☐ Other :	☐ Other :			

Witness Full name :	Phone number :
Email Address :	Witness Signature:
Address :	

Document Type	Date/Time Notarized	Document Type	Fee Charged
			Record Number

NOTARY RECORD

Full name :	Phone number :	Thumb print :
Email Address :	Signature :	
Address :	Signer's Signature	

Service Performed	Identification		ID Number :	
☐ Jurat	☐ ID Card	☐ Credible Witness		
☐ Oath	☐ Passport	☐ Known Personally	Issued by :	
☐ Acknowledgement	☐ Drivers License		Date Issued :	Expiration Date:
☐ Other :	☐ Other :			

Witness Full name :	Phone number :
Email Address :	Witness Signature:
Address :	

Document Type	Date/Time Notarized	Document Type	Fee Charged
			Record Number

NOTES

NOTARY RECORD

Full name :	Phone number :	Thumb print :
Email Address : Address :	Signature : Signer's Signature	

Service Performed ☐ Jurat ☐ Oath ☐ Acknowledgement ☐ Other :	Identification ☐ ID Card ☐ Credible Witness ☐ Passport ☐ Known Personally ☐ Drivers License ☐ Other :	ID Number : Issued by :
		Date Issued :	Expiration Date:

Witness Full name :	Phone number :
Email Address : Address :	Witness Signature:

Document Type	Date/Time Notarized	Document Type	Fee Charged
			Record Number

NOTARY RECORD

Full name :	Phone number :	Thumb print :
Email Address : Address :	Signature : Signer's Signature	

Service Performed ☐ Jurat ☐ Oath ☐ Acknowledgement ☐ Other :	Identification ☐ ID Card ☐ Credible Witness ☐ Passport ☐ Known Personally ☐ Drivers License ☐ Other :	ID Number : Issued by :
		Date Issued :	Expiration Date:

Witness Full name :	Phone number :
Email Address : Address :	Witness Signature:

Document Type	Date/Time Notarized	Document Type	Fee Charged
			Record Number

NOTES

NOTARY RECORD

Full name :	Phone number :	Thumb print :
Email Address :	Signature :	
Address :	**Signer's Signature**	

Service Performed	Identification		ID Number :	
☐ Jurat	☐ ID Card	☐ Credible Witness		
☐ Oath	☐ Passport	☐ Known Personally	Issued by :	
☐ Acknowledgement	☐ Drivers License		Date Issued :	Expiration Date:
☐ Other :	☐ Other :			

Witness Full name :	Phone number :	
Email Address :	Witness Signature:	
Address :		

Document Type	Date/Time Notarized	Document Type	Fee Charged
			Record Number

NOTARY RECORD

Full name :	Phone number :	Thumb print :
Email Address :	Signature :	
Address :	**Signer's Signature**	

Service Performed	Identification		ID Number :	
☐ Jurat	☐ ID Card	☐ Credible Witness		
☐ Oath	☐ Passport	☐ Known Personally	Issued by :	
☐ Acknowledgement	☐ Drivers License		Date Issued :	Expiration Date:
☐ Other :	☐ Other :			

Witness Full name :	Phone number :	
Email Address :	Witness Signature:	
Address :		

Document Type	Date/Time Notarized	Document Type	Fee Charged
			Record Number

NOTES

NOTARY RECORD

Full name :	Phone number :	Thumb print :
Email Address :	Signature :	
Address :	**Signer's Signature**	

Service Performed	Identification		ID Number :	
☐ Jurat	☐ ID Card	☐ Credible Witness		
☐ Oath	☐ Passport	☐ Known Personally	Issued by :	
☐ Acknowledgement	☐ Drivers License		Date Issued :	Expiration Date:
☐ Other :	☐ Other :			

Witness Full name :	Phone number :
Email Address :	Witness Signature:
Address :	

Document Type	Date/Time Notarized	Document Type	Fee Charged
			Record Number

NOTARY RECORD

Full name :	Phone number :	Thumb print :
Email Address :	Signature :	
Address :	**Signer's Signature**	

Service Performed	Identification		ID Number :	
☐ Jurat	☐ ID Card	☐ Credible Witness		
☐ Oath	☐ Passport	☐ Known Personally	Issued by :	
☐ Acknowledgement	☐ Drivers License		Date Issued :	Expiration Date:
☐ Other :	☐ Other :			

Witness Full name :	Phone number :
Email Address :	Witness Signature:
Address :	

Document Type	Date/Time Notarized	Document Type	Fee Charged
			Record Number

NOTES

NOTARY RECORD

Full name :	Phone number :	Thumb print :
Email Address :	Signature :	
Address :	**Signer's Signature**	

Service Performed	Identification		ID Number :	
☐ Jurat	☐ ID Card	☐ Credible Witness		
☐ Oath	☐ Passport	☐ Known Personally	Issued by :	
☐ Acknowledgement	☐ Drivers License		Date Issued :	Expiration Date:
☐ Other :	☐ Other :			

Witness Full name :	Phone number :
Email Address :	Witness Signature:
Address :	

Document Type	Date/Time Notarized	Document Type	Fee Charged
			Record Number

NOTARY RECORD

Full name :	Phone number :	Thumb print :
Email Address :	Signature :	
Address :	**Signer's Signature**	

Service Performed	Identification		ID Number :	
☐ Jurat	☐ ID Card	☐ Credible Witness		
☐ Oath	☐ Passport	☐ Known Personally	Issued by :	
☐ Acknowledgement	☐ Drivers License		Date Issued :	Expiration Date:
☐ Other :	☐ Other :			

Witness Full name :	Phone number :
Email Address :	Witness Signature:
Address :	

Document Type	Date/Time Notarized	Document Type	Fee Charged
			Record Number

NOTES

NOTARY RECORD

Full name :	Phone number :	Thumb print :
Email Address : Address :	Signature : **Signer's Signature**	

Service Performed ☐ Jurat ☐ Oath ☐ Acknowledgement ☐ Other :	Identification ☐ ID Card ☐ Passport ☐ Drivers License ☐ Other :	☐ Credible Witness ☐ Known Personally	ID Number :	
			Issued by :	
			Date Issued :	Expiration Date:

Witness Full name :	Phone number :
Email Address : Address :	Witness Signature:

Document Type	Date/Time Notarized	Document Type	Fee Charged
			Record Number

NOTARY RECORD

Full name :	Phone number :	Thumb print :
Email Address : Address :	Signature : **Signer's Signature**	

Service Performed ☐ Jurat ☐ Oath ☐ Acknowledgement ☐ Other :	Identification ☐ ID Card ☐ Passport ☐ Drivers License ☐ Other :	☐ Credible Witness ☐ Known Personally	ID Number :	
			Issued by :	
			Date Issued :	Expiration Date:

Witness Full name :	Phone number :
Email Address : Address :	Witness Signature:

Document Type	Date/Time Notarized	Document Type	Fee Charged
			Record Number

NOTES

NOTARY RECORD

Full name :	Phone number :	Thumb print :
Email Address :	Signature :	
Address :	**Signer's Signature**	

Service Performed	Identification	ID Number :	
☐ Jurat	☐ ID Card ☐ Credible Witness		
☐ Oath	☐ Passport ☐ Known Personally	Issued by :	
☐ Acknowledgement	☐ Drivers License		
☐ Other :	☐ Other :	Date Issued :	Expiration Date:

Witness Full name :	Phone number :
Email Address :	Witness Signature:
Address :	

Document Type	Date/Time Notarized	Document Type	Fee Charged
			Record Number

NOTARY RECORD

Full name :	Phone number :	Thumb print :
Email Address :	Signature :	
Address :	**Signer's Signature**	

Service Performed	Identification	ID Number :	
☐ Jurat	☐ ID Card ☐ Credible Witness		
☐ Oath	☐ Passport ☐ Known Personally	Issued by :	
☐ Acknowledgement	☐ Drivers License		
☐ Other :	☐ Other :	Date Issued :	Expiration Date:

Witness Full name :	Phone number :
Email Address :	Witness Signature:
Address :	

Document Type	Date/Time Notarized	Document Type	Fee Charged
			Record Number

NOTES

NOTARY RECORD

Full name :	Phone number :	Thumb print :
Email Address :	Signature :	
Address :	**Signer's Signature**	

Service Performed	Identification		ID Number :	
☐ Jurat	☐ ID Card	☐ Credible Witness		
☐ Oath	☐ Passport	☐ Known Personally	Issued by :	
☐ Acknowledgement	☐ Drivers License			
☐ Other :	☐ Other :		Date Issued :	Expiration Date:

Witness Full name :	Phone number :
Email Address :	Witness Signature:
Address :	

Document Type	Date/Time Notarized	Document Type	Fee Charged
			Record Number

NOTARY RECORD

Full name :	Phone number :	Thumb print :
Email Address :	Signature :	
Address :	**Signer's Signature**	

Service Performed	Identification		ID Number :	
☐ Jurat	☐ ID Card	☐ Credible Witness		
☐ Oath	☐ Passport	☐ Known Personally	Issued by :	
☐ Acknowledgement	☐ Drivers License			
☐ Other :	☐ Other :		Date Issued :	Expiration Date:

Witness Full name :	Phone number :
Email Address :	Witness Signature:
Address :	

Document Type	Date/Time Notarized	Document Type	Fee Charged
			Record Number

NOTES

NOTARY RECORD

Full name :	Phone number :	Thumb print :
Email Address :	Signature : **Signer's Signature**	
Address :		

Service Performed	Identification		ID Number :	
☐ Jurat	☐ ID Card	☐ Credible Witness		
☐ Oath	☐ Passport	☐ Known Personally	Issued by :	
☐ Acknowledgement	☐ Drivers License			
☐ Other :	☐ Other :		Date Issued :	Expiration Date:

Witness Full name :	Phone number :
Email Address :	Witness Signature:
Address :	

Document Type	Date/Time Notarized	Document Type	Fee Charged
			Record Number

NOTARY RECORD

Full name :	Phone number :	Thumb print :
Email Address :	Signature : **Signer's Signature**	
Address :		

Service Performed	Identification		ID Number :	
☐ Jurat	☐ ID Card	☐ Credible Witness		
☐ Oath	☐ Passport	☐ Known Personally	Issued by :	
☐ Acknowledgement	☐ Drivers License			
☐ Other :	☐ Other :		Date Issued :	Expiration Date:

Witness Full name :	Phone number :
Email Address :	Witness Signature:
Address :	

Document Type	Date/Time Notarized	Document Type	Fee Charged
			Record Number

NOTES

NOTARY RECORD

Full name :	Phone number :	Thumb print :
Email Address :	Signature :	
Address :	**Signer's Signature**	

Service Performed	Identification		ID Number :
☐ Jurat	☐ ID Card	☐ Credible Witness	
☐ Oath	☐ Passport	☐ Known Personally	Issued by :
☐ Acknowledgement	☐ Drivers License		
☐ Other :	☐ Other :	Date Issued :	Expiration Date:

Witness Full name :	Phone number :
Email Address :	Witness Signature:
Address :	

Document Type	Date/Time Notarized	Document Type	Fee Charged
			Record Number

NOTARY RECORD

Full name :	Phone number :	Thumb print :
Email Address :	Signature :	
Address :	**Signer's Signature**	

Service Performed	Identification		ID Number :
☐ Jurat	☐ ID Card	☐ Credible Witness	
☐ Oath	☐ Passport	☐ Known Personally	Issued by :
☐ Acknowledgement	☐ Drivers License		
☐ Other :	☐ Other :	Date Issued :	Expiration Date:

Witness Full name :	Phone number :
Email Address :	Witness Signature:
Address :	

Document Type	Date/Time Notarized	Document Type	Fee Charged
			Record Number

NOTES

NOTARY RECORD

Full name :	Phone number :	Thumb print :
Email Address :	Signature :	
Address :	Signer's Signature	

Service Performed	Identification		ID Number :	
☐ Jurat	☐ ID Card	☐ Credible Witness		
☐ Oath	☐ Passport	☐ Known Personally	Issued by :	
☐ Acknowledgement	☐ Drivers License		Date Issued :	Expiration Date:
☐ Other :	☐ Other :			

Witness Full name :	Phone number :
Email Address :	Witness Signature:
Address :	

Document Type	Date/Time Notarized	Document Type	Fee Charged
			Record Number

NOTARY RECORD

Full name :	Phone number :	Thumb print :
Email Address :	Signature :	
Address :	Signer's Signature	

Service Performed	Identification		ID Number :	
☐ Jurat	☐ ID Card	☐ Credible Witness		
☐ Oath	☐ Passport	☐ Known Personally	Issued by :	
☐ Acknowledgement	☐ Drivers License		Date Issued :	Expiration Date:
☐ Other :	☐ Other :			

Witness Full name :	Phone number :
Email Address :	Witness Signature:
Address :	

Document Type	Date/Time Notarized	Document Type	Fee Charged
			Record Number

NOTES

NOTARY RECORD

Full name :	Phone number :	Thumb print :
Email Address :	Signature :	
Address :	Signer's Signature	

Service Performed	Identification		ID Number :
☐ Jurat	☐ ID Card	☐ Credible Witness	
☐ Oath	☐ Passport	☐ Known Personally	Issued by :
☐ Acknowledgement	☐ Drivers License		
☐ Other :	☐ Other :		Date Issued :	Expiration Date:

Witness Full name :	Phone number :
Email Address :	Witness Signature:
Address :	

Document Type	Date/Time Notarized	Document Type	Fee Charged
			Record Number

NOTARY RECORD

Full name :	Phone number :	Thumb print :
Email Address :	Signature :	
Address :	Signer's Signature	

Service Performed	Identification		ID Number :
☐ Jurat	☐ ID Card	☐ Credible Witness	
☐ Oath	☐ Passport	☐ Known Personally	Issued by :
☐ Acknowledgement	☐ Drivers License		
☐ Other :	☐ Other :		Date Issued :	Expiration Date:

Witness Full name :	Phone number :
Email Address :	Witness Signature:
Address :	

Document Type	Date/Time Notarized	Document Type	Fee Charged
			Record Number

NOTES

NOTARY RECORD

Full name :	Phone number :	Thumb print :
Email Address :	Signature :	
Address :	**Signer's Signature**	

Service Performed	Identification		ID Number :	
☐ Jurat	☐ ID Card	☐ Credible Witness		
☐ Oath	☐ Passport	☐ Known Personally	Issued by :	
☐ Acknowledgement	☐ Drivers License			
☐ Other :	☐ Other :		Date Issued :	Expiration Date:

Witness Full name :		Phone number :	
Email Address :		Witness Signature:	
Address :			

Document Type	Date/Time Notarized	Document Type	Fee Charged
			Record Number

NOTARY RECORD

Full name :	Phone number :	Thumb print :
Email Address :	Signature :	
Address :	**Signer's Signature**	

Service Performed	Identification		ID Number :	
☐ Jurat	☐ ID Card	☐ Credible Witness		
☐ Oath	☐ Passport	☐ Known Personally	Issued by :	
☐ Acknowledgement	☐ Drivers License			
☐ Other :	☐ Other :		Date Issued :	Expiration Date:

Witness Full name :		Phone number :	
Email Address :		Witness Signature:	
Address :			

Document Type	Date/Time Notarized	Document Type	Fee Charged
			Record Number

NOTES

NOTARY RECORD

Full name :	Phone number :	Thumb print :
Email Address : Address :	Signature : **Signer's Signature**	

Service Performed ☐ Jurat ☐ Oath ☐ Acknowledgement ☐ Other :	Identification ☐ ID Card ☐ Credible Witness ☐ Passport ☐ Known Personally ☐ Drivers License ☐ Other :	ID Number : Issued by : Date Issued : Expiration Date:

Witness Full name :	Phone number :
Email Address : Address :	Witness Signature:

Document Type	Date/Time Notarized	Document Type	Fee Charged
			Record Number

NOTARY RECORD

Full name :	Phone number :	Thumb print :
Email Address : Address :	Signature : **Signer's Signature**	

Service Performed ☐ Jurat ☐ Oath ☐ Acknowledgement ☐ Other :	Identification ☐ ID Card ☐ Credible Witness ☐ Passport ☐ Known Personally ☐ Drivers License ☐ Other :	ID Number : Issued by : Date Issued : Expiration Date:

Witness Full name :	Phone number :
Email Address : Address :	Witness Signature:

Document Type	Date/Time Notarized	Document Type	Fee Charged
			Record Number

NOTES

NOTARY RECORD

Full name :	Phone number :	Thumb print :
Email Address :	Signature :	
Address :	Signer's Signature	

Service Performed	Identification		ID Number :	
☐ Jurat	☐ ID Card	☐ Credible Witness		
☐ Oath	☐ Passport	☐ Known Personally	Issued by :	
☐ Acknowledgement	☐ Drivers License		Date Issued :	Expiration Date:
☐ Other :	☐ Other :			

Witness Full name :	Phone number :
Email Address :	Witness Signature:
Address :	

Document Type	Date/Time Notarized	Document Type	Fee Charged
			Record Number

NOTARY RECORD

Full name :	Phone number :	Thumb print :
Email Address :	Signature :	
Address :	Signer's Signature	

Service Performed	Identification		ID Number :	
☐ Jurat	☐ ID Card	☐ Credible Witness		
☐ Oath	☐ Passport	☐ Known Personally	Issued by :	
☐ Acknowledgement	☐ Drivers License		Date Issued :	Expiration Date:
☐ Other :	☐ Other :			

Witness Full name :	Phone number :
Email Address :	Witness Signature:
Address :	

Document Type	Date/Time Notarized	Document Type	Fee Charged
			Record Number

NOTES

NOTARY RECORD

Full name :	Phone number :	Thumb print :
Email Address :	Signature : Signer's Signature	
Address :		

Service Performed	Identification		ID Number :
☐ Jurat	☐ ID Card	☐ Credible Witness	
☐ Oath	☐ Passport	☐ Known Personally	Issued by :
☐ Acknowledgement	☐ Drivers License		Date Issued : Expiration Date:
☐ Other :	☐ Other :		

Witness Full name :	Phone number :
Email Address :	Witness Signature:
Address :	

Document Type	Date/Time Notarized	Document Type	Fee Charged
			Record Number

NOTARY RECORD

Full name :	Phone number :	Thumb print :
Email Address :	Signature : Signer's Signature	
Address :		

Service Performed	Identification		ID Number :
☐ Jurat	☐ ID Card	☐ Credible Witness	
☐ Oath	☐ Passport	☐ Known Personally	Issued by :
☐ Acknowledgement	☐ Drivers License		Date Issued : Expiration Date:
☐ Other :	☐ Other :		

Witness Full name :	Phone number :
Email Address :	Witness Signature:
Address :	

Document Type	Date/Time Notarized	Document Type	Fee Charged
			Record Number

NOTES

NOTARY RECORD

Full name :	Phone number :	Thumb print :
Email Address :	Signature :	
Address :	**Signer's Signature**	

Service Performed	Identification		ID Number :	
☐ Jurat	☐ ID Card	☐ Credible Witness		
☐ Oath	☐ Passport	☐ Known Personally	Issued by :	
☐ Acknowledgement	☐ Drivers License			
☐ Other :	☐ Other :		Date Issued :	Expiration Date:

Witness Full name :	Phone number :
Email Address :	Witness Signature:
Address :	

Document Type	Date/Time Notarized	Document Type	Fee Charged
			Record Number

NOTARY RECORD

Full name :	Phone number :	Thumb print :
Email Address :	Signature :	
Address :	**Signer's Signature**	

Service Performed	Identification		ID Number :	
☐ Jurat	☐ ID Card	☐ Credible Witness		
☐ Oath	☐ Passport	☐ Known Personally	Issued by :	
☐ Acknowledgement	☐ Drivers License			
☐ Other :	☐ Other :		Date Issued :	Expiration Date:

Witness Full name :	Phone number :
Email Address :	Witness Signature:
Address :	

Document Type	Date/Time Notarized	Document Type	Fee Charged
			Record Number

NOTES

NOTARY RECORD

Full name :	Phone number :	Thumb print :
Email Address :	Signature :	
Address :	Signer's Signature	

Service Performed	Identification		ID Number :	
☐ Jurat	☐ ID Card	☐ Credible Witness		
☐ Oath	☐ Passport	☐ Known Personally	Issued by :	
☐ Acknowledgement	☐ Drivers License		Date Issued :	Expiration Date:
☐ Other :	☐ Other :			

Witness Full name :	Phone number :
Email Address :	Witness Signature:
Address :	

Document Type	Date/Time Notarized	Document Type	Fee Charged
			Record Number

NOTARY RECORD

Full name :	Phone number :	Thumb print :
Email Address :	Signature :	
Address :	Signer's Signature	

Service Performed	Identification		ID Number :	
☐ Jurat	☐ ID Card	☐ Credible Witness		
☐ Oath	☐ Passport	☐ Known Personally	Issued by :	
☐ Acknowledgement	☐ Drivers License		Date Issued :	Expiration Date:
☐ Other :	☐ Other :			

Witness Full name :	Phone number :
Email Address :	Witness Signature:
Address :	

Document Type	Date/Time Notarized	Document Type	Fee Charged
			Record Number

NOTES

NOTARY RECORD

Full name :	Phone number :	Thumb print :
Email Address :	Signature :	
Address :	**Signer's Signature**	

Service Performed	Identification		ID Number :	
☐ Jurat	☐ ID Card	☐ Credible Witness		
☐ Oath	☐ Passport	☐ Known Personally	Issued by :	
☐ Acknowledgement	☐ Drivers License		Date Issued :	Expiration Date:
☐ Other :	☐ Other :			

Witness Full name :	Phone number :
Email Address :	Witness Signature:
Address :	

Document Type	Date/Time Notarized	Document Type	Fee Charged
			Record Number

NOTARY RECORD

Full name :	Phone number :	Thumb print :
Email Address :	Signature :	
Address :	**Signer's Signature**	

Service Performed	Identification		ID Number :	
☐ Jurat	☐ ID Card	☐ Credible Witness		
☐ Oath	☐ Passport	☐ Known Personally	Issued by :	
☐ Acknowledgement	☐ Drivers License		Date Issued :	Expiration Date:
☐ Other :	☐ Other :			

Witness Full name :	Phone number :
Email Address :	Witness Signature:
Address :	

Document Type	Date/Time Notarized	Document Type	Fee Charged
			Record Number

NOTES

NOTARY RECORD

Full name :	Phone number :	Thumb print :
Email Address :	Signature :	
Address :	Signer's Signature	

Service Performed	Identification		ID Number :	
☐ Jurat	☐ ID Card	☐ Credible Witness		
☐ Oath	☐ Passport	☐ Known Personally	Issued by :	
☐ Acknowledgement	☐ Drivers License		Date Issued :	Expiration Date:
☐ Other :	☐ Other :			

Witness Full name :	Phone number :
Email Address :	Witness Signature:
Address :	

Document Type	Date/Time Notarized	Document Type	Fee Charged
			Record Number

NOTARY RECORD

Full name :	Phone number :	Thumb print :
Email Address :	Signature :	
Address :	Signer's Signature	

Service Performed	Identification		ID Number :	
☐ Jurat	☐ ID Card	☐ Credible Witness		
☐ Oath	☐ Passport	☐ Known Personally	Issued by :	
☐ Acknowledgement	☐ Drivers License		Date Issued :	Expiration Date:
☐ Other :	☐ Other :			

Witness Full name :	Phone number :
Email Address :	Witness Signature:
Address :	

Document Type	Date/Time Notarized	Document Type	Fee Charged
			Record Number

NOTES

NOTARY RECORD

Full name :	Phone number :	Thumb print :
Email Address :	Signature :	
Address :	**Signer's Signature**	

Service Performed	Identification		ID Number :	
☐ Jurat	☐ ID Card	☐ Credible Witness		
☐ Oath	☐ Passport	☐ Known Personally	Issued by :	
☐ Acknowledgement	☐ Drivers License		Date Issued :	Expiration Date:
☐ Other :	☐ Other :			

Witness Full name :	Phone number :
Email Address :	Witness Signature:
Address :	

Document Type	Date/Time Notarized	Document Type	Fee Charged
			Record Number

NOTARY RECORD

Full name :	Phone number :	Thumb print :
Email Address :	Signature :	
Address :	**Signer's Signature**	

Service Performed	Identification		ID Number :	
☐ Jurat	☐ ID Card	☐ Credible Witness		
☐ Oath	☐ Passport	☐ Known Personally	Issued by :	
☐ Acknowledgement	☐ Drivers License		Date Issued :	Expiration Date:
☐ Other :	☐ Other :			

Witness Full name :	Phone number :
Email Address :	Witness Signature:
Address :	

Document Type	Date/Time Notarized	Document Type	Fee Charged
			Record Number

NOTES

NOTARY RECORD

Full name :	Phone number :	Thumb print :
Email Address :	Signature :	
Address :	Signer's Signature	

Service Performed	Identification		ID Number :	
☐ Jurat	☐ ID Card	☐ Credible Witness		
☐ Oath	☐ Passport	☐ Known Personally	Issued by :	
☐ Acknowledgement	☐ Drivers License		Date Issued :	Expiration Date:
☐ Other :	☐ Other :			

Witness Full name :	Phone number :
Email Address :	Witness Signature:
Address :	

Document Type	Date/Time Notarized	Document Type	Fee Charged
			Record Number

NOTARY RECORD

Full name :	Phone number :	Thumb print :
Email Address :	Signature :	
Address :	Signer's Signature	

Service Performed	Identification		ID Number :	
☐ Jurat	☐ ID Card	☐ Credible Witness		
☐ Oath	☐ Passport	☐ Known Personally	Issued by :	
☐ Acknowledgement	☐ Drivers License		Date Issued :	Expiration Date:
☐ Other :	☐ Other :			

Witness Full name :	Phone number :
Email Address :	Witness Signature:
Address :	

Document Type	Date/Time Notarized	Document Type	Fee Charged
			Record Number

NOTES

NOTARY RECORD

Full name :	Phone number :	Thumb print :
Email Address : Address :	Signature : **Signer's Signature**	

Service Performed	Identification		ID Number :	
☐ Jurat	☐ ID Card	☐ Credible Witness		
☐ Oath	☐ Passport	☐ Known Personally	Issued by :	
☐ Acknowledgement	☐ Drivers License		Date Issued :	Expiration Date:
☐ Other :	☐ Other :			

Witness Full name :	Phone number :
Email Address : Address :	Witness Signature:

Document Type	Date/Time Notarized	Document Type	Fee Charged
			Record Number

NOTARY RECORD

Full name :	Phone number :	Thumb print :
Email Address : Address :	Signature : **Signer's Signature**	

Service Performed	Identification		ID Number :	
☐ Jurat	☐ ID Card	☐ Credible Witness		
☐ Oath	☐ Passport	☐ Known Personally	Issued by :	
☐ Acknowledgement	☐ Drivers License		Date Issued :	Expiration Date:
☐ Other :	☐ Other :			

Witness Full name :	Phone number :
Email Address : Address :	Witness Signature:

Document Type	Date/Time Notarized	Document Type	Fee Charged
			Record Number

NOTES

NOTARY RECORD

Full name :		Phone number :	Thumb print :
Email Address :		Signature :	
Address :		Signer's Signature	

Service Performed	Identification		ID Number :	
☐ Jurat	☐ ID Card	☐ Credible Witness		
☐ Oath	☐ Passport	☐ Known Personally	Issued by :	
☐ Acknowledgement	☐ Drivers License		Date Issued :	Expiration Date:
☐ Other :	☐ Other :			

Witness Full name :		Phone number :
Email Address :		Witness Signature:
Address :		

Document Type	Date/Time Notarized	Document Type	Fee Charged
			Record Number

NOTARY RECORD

Full name :		Phone number :	Thumb print :
Email Address :		Signature :	
Address :		Signer's Signature	

Service Performed	Identification		ID Number :	
☐ Jurat	☐ ID Card	☐ Credible Witness		
☐ Oath	☐ Passport	☐ Known Personally	Issued by :	
☐ Acknowledgement	☐ Drivers License		Date Issued :	Expiration Date:
☐ Other :	☐ Other :			

Witness Full name :		Phone number :
Email Address :		Witness Signature:
Address :		

Document Type	Date/Time Notarized	Document Type	Fee Charged
			Record Number

NOTES

NOTARY RECORD

Full name :	Phone number :	Thumb print :
Email Address :	Signature :	
Address :	**Signer's Signature**	

Service Performed	Identification		ID Number :	
☐ Jurat	☐ ID Card	☐ Credible Witness		
☐ Oath	☐ Passport	☐ Known Personally	Issued by :	
☐ Acknowledgement	☐ Drivers License			
☐ Other :	☐ Other :		Date Issued :	Expiration Date:

Witness Full name :	Phone number :
Email Address :	Witness Signature:
Address :	

Document Type	Date/Time Notarized	Document Type	Fee Charged
			Record Number

NOTARY RECORD

Full name :	Phone number :	Thumb print :
Email Address :	Signature :	
Address :	**Signer's Signature**	

Service Performed	Identification		ID Number :	
☐ Jurat	☐ ID Card	☐ Credible Witness		
☐ Oath	☐ Passport	☐ Known Personally	Issued by :	
☐ Acknowledgement	☐ Drivers License			
☐ Other :	☐ Other :		Date Issued :	Expiration Date:

Witness Full name :	Phone number :
Email Address :	Witness Signature:
Address :	

Document Type	Date/Time Notarized	Document Type	Fee Charged
			Record Number

NOTES

NOTARY RECORD

Full name :	Phone number :	Thumb print :
Email Address :	Signature : **Signer's Signature**	
Address :		

Service Performed ☐ Jurat ☐ Oath ☐ Acknowledgement ☐ Other :	Identification ☐ ID Card ☐ Credible Witness ☐ Passport ☐ Known Personally ☐ Drivers License ☐ Other :	ID Number :
		Issued by :
		Date Issued : / Expiration Date:

Witness Full name :	Phone number :
Email Address :	Witness Signature:
Address :	

Document Type	Date/Time Notarized	Document Type	Fee Charged
			Record Number

NOTARY RECORD

Full name :	Phone number :	Thumb print :
Email Address :	Signature : **Signer's Signature**	
Address :		

Service Performed ☐ Jurat ☐ Oath ☐ Acknowledgement ☐ Other :	Identification ☐ ID Card ☐ Credible Witness ☐ Passport ☐ Known Personally ☐ Drivers License ☐ Other :	ID Number :
		Issued by :
		Date Issued : / Expiration Date:

Witness Full name :	Phone number :
Email Address :	Witness Signature:
Address :	

Document Type	Date/Time Notarized	Document Type	Fee Charged
			Record Number

NOTES

NOTARY RECORD

Full name :	Phone number :	Thumb print :
Email Address :	Signature :	
Address :	Signer's Signature	

Service Performed	Identification	ID Number :	
☐ Jurat	☐ ID Card ☐ Credible Witness		
☐ Oath	☐ Passport ☐ Known Personally	Issued by :	
☐ Acknowledgement	☐ Drivers License	Date Issued :	Expiration Date:
☐ Other :	☐ Other :		

Witness Full name :	Phone number :
Email Address :	Witness Signature:
Address :	

Document Type	Date/Time Notarized	Document Type	Fee Charged
			Record Number

NOTARY RECORD

Full name :	Phone number :	Thumb print :
Email Address :	Signature :	
Address :	Signer's Signature	

Service Performed	Identification	ID Number :	
☐ Jurat	☐ ID Card ☐ Credible Witness		
☐ Oath	☐ Passport ☐ Known Personally	Issued by :	
☐ Acknowledgement	☐ Drivers License	Date Issued :	Expiration Date:
☐ Other :	☐ Other :		

Witness Full name :	Phone number :
Email Address :	Witness Signature:
Address :	

Document Type	Date/Time Notarized	Document Type	Fee Charged
			Record Number

NOTES

NOTARY RECORD

Full name :	Phone number :	Thumb print :
Email Address : Address :	Signature : **Signer's Signature**	

Service Performed ☐ Jurat ☐ Oath ☐ Acknowledgement ☐ Other :	Identification ☐ ID Card ☐ Passport ☐ Drivers License ☐ Other :	☐ Credible Witness ☐ Known Personally	ID Number :	
			Issued by :	
			Date Issued :	Expiration Date:

Witness Full name :	Phone number :
Email Address : Address :	Witness Signature:

Document Type	Date/Time Notarized	Document Type	Fee Charged
			Record Number

NOTARY RECORD

Full name :	Phone number :	Thumb print :
Email Address : Address :	Signature : **Signer's Signature**	

Service Performed ☐ Jurat ☐ Oath ☐ Acknowledgement ☐ Other :	Identification ☐ ID Card ☐ Passport ☐ Drivers License ☐ Other :	☐ Credible Witness ☐ Known Personally	ID Number :	
			Issued by :	
			Date Issued :	Expiration Date:

Witness Full name :	Phone number :
Email Address : Address :	Witness Signature:

Document Type	Date/Time Notarized	Document Type	Fee Charged
			Record Number

NOTES

NOTARY RECORD

Full name :	Phone number :	Thumb print :
Email Address :	Signature :	
Address :	Signer's Signature	

Service Performed	Identification		ID Number :	
☐ Jurat	☐ ID Card	☐ Credible Witness		
☐ Oath	☐ Passport	☐ Known Personally	Issued by :	
☐ Acknowledgement	☐ Drivers License		Date Issued :	Expiration Date:
☐ Other :	☐ Other :			

Witness Full name :	Phone number :
Email Address :	Witness Signature:
Address :	

Document Type	Date/Time Notarized	Document Type	Fee Charged
			Record Number

NOTARY RECORD

Full name :	Phone number :	Thumb print :
Email Address :	Signature :	
Address :	Signer's Signature	

Service Performed	Identification		ID Number :	
☐ Jurat	☐ ID Card	☐ Credible Witness		
☐ Oath	☐ Passport	☐ Known Personally	Issued by :	
☐ Acknowledgement	☐ Drivers License		Date Issued :	Expiration Date:
☐ Other :	☐ Other :			

Witness Full name :	Phone number :
Email Address :	Witness Signature:
Address :	

Document Type	Date/Time Notarized	Document Type	Fee Charged
			Record Number

NOTES

NOTARY RECORD

Full name :	Phone number :	Thumb print :
Email Address :	Signature : Signer's Signature	
Address :		

Service Performed	Identification		ID Number :	
☐ Jurat	☐ ID Card	☐ Credible Witness		
☐ Oath	☐ Passport	☐ Known Personally	Issued by :	
☐ Acknowledgement	☐ Drivers License		Date Issued :	Expiration Date:
☐ Other :	☐ Other :			

Witness Full name :		Phone number :	
Email Address :		Witness Signature:	
Address :			

Document Type	Date/Time Notarized	Document Type	Fee Charged
			Record Number

NOTARY RECORD

Full name :	Phone number :	Thumb print :
Email Address :	Signature : Signer's Signature	
Address :		

Service Performed	Identification		ID Number :	
☐ Jurat	☐ ID Card	☐ Credible Witness		
☐ Oath	☐ Passport	☐ Known Personally	Issued by :	
☐ Acknowledgement	☐ Drivers License		Date Issued :	Expiration Date:
☐ Other :	☐ Other :			

Witness Full name :		Phone number :	
Email Address :		Witness Signature:	
Address :			

Document Type	Date/Time Notarized	Document Type	Fee Charged
			Record Number

NOTES

NOTARY RECORD

Full name :	Phone number :	Thumb print :
Email Address :	Signature :	
Address :	Signer's Signature	

Service Performed	Identification		ID Number :	
☐ Jurat	☐ ID Card	☐ Credible Witness		
☐ Oath	☐ Passport	☐ Known Personally	Issued by :	
☐ Acknowledgement	☐ Drivers License		Date Issued :	Expiration Date:
☐ Other :	☐ Other :			

Witness Full name :		Phone number :	
Email Address :		Witness Signature:	
Address :			

Document Type	Date/Time Notarized	Document Type	Fee Charged
			Record Number

NOTARY RECORD

Full name :	Phone number :	Thumb print :
Email Address :	Signature :	
Address :	Signer's Signature	

Service Performed	Identification		ID Number :	
☐ Jurat	☐ ID Card	☐ Credible Witness		
☐ Oath	☐ Passport	☐ Known Personally	Issued by :	
☐ Acknowledgement	☐ Drivers License		Date Issued :	Expiration Date:
☐ Other :	☐ Other :			

Witness Full name :		Phone number :	
Email Address :		Witness Signature:	
Address :			

Document Type	Date/Time Notarized	Document Type	Fee Charged
			Record Number

NOTES

NOTARY RECORD

Full name :	Phone number :	Thumb print :
Email Address :	Signature :	
Address :	Signer's Signature	

Service Performed	Identification		ID Number :	
☐ Jurat	☐ ID Card	☐ Credible Witness		
☐ Oath	☐ Passport	☐ Known Personally	Issued by :	
☐ Acknowledgement	☐ Drivers License		Date Issued :	Expiration Date:
☐ Other :	☐ Other :			

Witness Full name :	Phone number :
Email Address :	Witness Signature:
Address :	

Document Type	Date/Time Notarized	Document Type	Fee Charged
			Record Number

NOTARY RECORD

Full name :	Phone number :	Thumb print :
Email Address :	Signature :	
Address :	Signer's Signature	

Service Performed	Identification		ID Number :	
☐ Jurat	☐ ID Card	☐ Credible Witness		
☐ Oath	☐ Passport	☐ Known Personally	Issued by :	
☐ Acknowledgement	☐ Drivers License		Date Issued :	Expiration Date:
☐ Other :	☐ Other :			

Witness Full name :	Phone number :
Email Address :	Witness Signature:
Address :	

Document Type	Date/Time Notarized	Document Type	Fee Charged
			Record Number

NOTES

NOTARY RECORD

Full name :	Phone number :	Thumb print :
Email Address :	Signature :	
Address :	Signer's Signature	

Service Performed	Identification		ID Number :	
☐ Jurat	☐ ID Card	☐ Credible Witness		
☐ Oath	☐ Passport	☐ Known Personally	Issued by :	
☐ Acknowledgement	☐ Drivers License		Date Issued :	Expiration Date:
☐ Other :	☐ Other :			

Witness Full name :	Phone number :
Email Address :	Witness Signature:
Address :	

Document Type	Date/Time Notarized	Document Type	Fee Charged
			Record Number

NOTARY RECORD

Full name :	Phone number :	Thumb print :
Email Address :	Signature :	
Address :	Signer's Signature	

Service Performed	Identification		ID Number :	
☐ Jurat	☐ ID Card	☐ Credible Witness		
☐ Oath	☐ Passport	☐ Known Personally	Issued by :	
☐ Acknowledgement	☐ Drivers License		Date Issued :	Expiration Date:
☐ Other :	☐ Other :			

Witness Full name :	Phone number :
Email Address :	Witness Signature:
Address :	

Document Type	Date/Time Notarized	Document Type	Fee Charged
			Record Number

NOTES

NOTARY RECORD

Full name :	Phone number :	Thumb print :
Email Address :	Signature : **Signer's Signature**	
Address :		

Service Performed	Identification		ID Number :	
☐ Jurat	☐ ID Card	☐ Credible Witness		
☐ Oath	☐ Passport	☐ Known Personally	Issued by :	
☐ Acknowledgement	☐ Drivers License		Date Issued :	Expiration Date:
☐ Other :	☐ Other :			

Witness Full name :	Phone number :
Email Address :	Witness Signature:
Address :	

Document Type	Date/Time Notarized	Document Type	Fee Charged
			Record Number

NOTARY RECORD

Full name :	Phone number :	Thumb print :
Email Address :	Signature : **Signer's Signature**	
Address :		

Service Performed	Identification		ID Number :	
☐ Jurat	☐ ID Card	☐ Credible Witness		
☐ Oath	☐ Passport	☐ Known Personally	Issued by :	
☐ Acknowledgement	☐ Drivers License		Date Issued :	Expiration Date:
☐ Other :	☐ Other :			

Witness Full name :	Phone number :
Email Address :	Witness Signature:
Address :	

Document Type	Date/Time Notarized	Document Type	Fee Charged
			Record Number

NOTES

NOTARY RECORD

Full name :	Phone number :	Thumb print :
Email Address :	Signature :	
Address :	Signer's Signature	

Service Performed	Identification		ID Number :	
☐ Jurat	☐ ID Card	☐ Credible Witness		
☐ Oath	☐ Passport	☐ Known Personally	Issued by :	
☐ Acknowledgement	☐ Drivers License		Date Issued :	Expiration Date:
☐ Other :	☐ Other :			

Witness Full name :	Phone number :
Email Address :	Witness Signature:
Address :	

Document Type	Date/Time Notarized	Document Type	Fee Charged
			Record Number

NOTARY RECORD

Full name :	Phone number :	Thumb print :
Email Address :	Signature :	
Address :	Signer's Signature	

Service Performed	Identification		ID Number :	
☐ Jurat	☐ ID Card	☐ Credible Witness		
☐ Oath	☐ Passport	☐ Known Personally	Issued by :	
☐ Acknowledgement	☐ Drivers License		Date Issued :	Expiration Date:
☐ Other :	☐ Other :			

Witness Full name :	Phone number :
Email Address :	Witness Signature:
Address :	

Document Type	Date/Time Notarized	Document Type	Fee Charged
			Record Number

NOTES

NOTARY RECORD

Full name :	Phone number :	Thumb print :
Email Address :	Signature :	
Address :	**Signer's Signature**	

Service Performed	Identification	ID Number :	
☐ Jurat	☐ ID Card ☐ Credible Witness		
☐ Oath	☐ Passport ☐ Known Personally	Issued by :	
☐ Acknowledgement	☐ Drivers License		
☐ Other :	☐ Other :	Date Issued :	Expiration Date:

Witness Full name :	Phone number :
Email Address :	Witness Signature:
Address :	

Document Type	Date/Time Notarized	Document Type	Fee Charged
			Record Number

NOTARY RECORD

Full name :	Phone number :	Thumb print :
Email Address :	Signature :	
Address :	**Signer's Signature**	

Service Performed	Identification	ID Number :	
☐ Jurat	☐ ID Card ☐ Credible Witness		
☐ Oath	☐ Passport ☐ Known Personally	Issued by :	
☐ Acknowledgement	☐ Drivers License		
☐ Other :	☐ Other :	Date Issued :	Expiration Date

Witness Full name :	Phone number :
Email Address :	Witness Signature:
Address :	

Document Type	Date/Time Notarized	Document Type	Fee Charged
			Record Number

NOTES

NOTARY RECORD

Full name :	Phone number :	Thumb print :
Email Address :	Signature :	
Address :	Signer's Signature	

Service Performed	Identification		ID Number :	
☐ Jurat	☐ ID Card	☐ Credible Witness		
☐ Oath	☐ Passport	☐ Known Personally	Issued by :	
☐ Acknowledgement	☐ Drivers License			
☐ Other :	☐ Other :		Date Issued :	Expiration Date:

Witness Full name :	Phone number :
Email Address :	Witness Signature:
Address :	

Document Type	Date/Time Notarized	Document Type	Fee Charged
			Record Number

NOTARY RECORD

Full name :	Phone number :	Thumb print :
Email Address :	Signature :	
Address :	Signer's Signature	

Service Performed	Identification		ID Number :	
☐ Jurat	☐ ID Card	☐ Credible Witness		
☐ Oath	☐ Passport	☐ Known Personally	Issued by :	
☐ Acknowledgement	☐ Drivers License			
☐ Other :	☐ Other :		Date Issued :	Expiration Date:

Witness Full name :	Phone number :
Email Address :	Witness Signature:
Address :	

Document Type	Date/Time Notarized	Document Type	Fee Charged
			Record Number

NOTES

NOTARY RECORD

Full name :	Phone number :	Thumb print :
Email Address :	Signature : **Signer's Signature**	
Address :		

Service Performed	Identification		ID Number :	
☐ Jurat	☐ ID Card	☐ Credible Witness		
☐ Oath	☐ Passport	☐ Known Personally	Issued by :	
☐ Acknowledgement	☐ Drivers License		Date Issued :	Expiration Date:
☐ Other :	☐ Other :			

Witness Full name :	Phone number :
Email Address :	Witness Signature:
Address :	

Document Type	Date/Time Notarized	Document Type	Fee Charged
			Record Number

NOTARY RECORD

Full name :	Phone number :	Thumb print :
Email Address :	Signature : **Signer's Signature**	
Address :		

Service Performed	Identification		ID Number :	
☐ Jurat	☐ ID Card	☐ Credible Witness		
☐ Oath	☐ Passport	☐ Known Personally	Issued by :	
☐ Acknowledgement	☐ Drivers License		Date Issued :	Expiration Date:
☐ Other :	☐ Other :			

Witness Full name :	Phone number :
Email Address :	Witness Signature:
Address :	

Document Type	Date/Time Notarized	Document Type	Fee Charged
			Record Number

NOTES

NOTARY RECORD

Full name :	Phone number :	Thumb print :
Email Address :	Signature :	
Address :	Signer's Signature	

Service Performed	Identification	ID Number :	
☐ Jurat	☐ ID Card ☐ Credible Witness		
☐ Oath	☐ Passport ☐ Known Personally	Issued by :	
☐ Acknowledgement	☐ Drivers License		
☐ Other :	☐ Other :	Date Issued :	Expiration Date:

Witness Full name :	Phone number :
Email Address :	Witness Signature:
Address :	

Document Type	Date/Time Notarized	Document Type	Fee Charged
			Record Number

NOTARY RECORD

Full name :	Phone number :	Thumb print :
Email Address :	Signature :	
Address :	Signer's Signature	

Service Performed	Identification	ID Number :	
☐ Jurat	☐ ID Card ☐ Credible Witness		
☐ Oath	☐ Passport ☐ Known Personally	Issued by :	
☐ Acknowledgement	☐ Drivers License		
☐ Other :	☐ Other :	Date Issued :	Expiration Date:

Witness Full name :	Phone number :
Email Address :	Witness Signature:
Address :	

Document Type	Date/Time Notarized	Document Type	Fee Charged
			Record Number

NOTES

NOTARY RECORD

Full name :	Phone number :	Thumb print :
Email Address :	Signature :	
Address :	**Signer's Signature**	

Service Performed	Identification		ID Number :	
☐ Jurat	☐ ID Card	☐ Credible Witness		
☐ Oath	☐ Passport	☐ Known Personally	Issued by :	
☐ Acknowledgement	☐ Drivers License		Date Issued :	Expiration Date:
☐ Other :	☐ Other :			

Witness Full name :	Phone number :	
Email Address :	Witness Signature:	
Address :		

Document Type	Date/Time Notarized	Document Type	Fee Charged
			Record Number

NOTARY RECORD

Full name :	Phone number :	Thumb print :
Email Address :	Signature :	
Address :	**Signer's Signature**	

Service Performed	Identification		ID Number :	
☐ Jurat	☐ ID Card	☐ Credible Witness		
☐ Oath	☐ Passport	☐ Known Personally	Issued by :	
☐ Acknowledgement	☐ Drivers License		Date Issued :	Expiration Date:
☐ Other :	☐ Other :			

Witness Full name :	Phone number :	
Email Address :	Witness Signature:	
Address :		

Document Type	Date/Time Notarized	Document Type	Fee Charged
			Record Number

NOTES

NOTARY RECORD

Full name :	Phone number :	Thumb print :
Email Address :	Signature :	
Address :	**Signer's Signature**	

Service Performed	Identification		ID Number :	
☐ Jurat	☐ ID Card	☐ Credible Witness		
☐ Oath	☐ Passport	☐ Known Personally	Issued by :	
☐ Acknowledgement	☐ Drivers License			
☐ Other :	☐ Other :		Date Issued :	Expiration Date:

Witness Full name :	Phone number :
Email Address :	Witness Signature:
Address :	

Document Type	Date/Time Notarized	Document Type	Fee Charged
			Record Number

NOTARY RECORD

Full name :	Phone number :	Thumb print :
Email Address :	Signature :	
Address :	**Signer's Signature**	

Service Performed	Identification		ID Number :	
☐ Jurat	☐ ID Card	☐ Credible Witness		
☐ Oath	☐ Passport	☐ Known Personally	Issued by :	
☐ Acknowledgement	☐ Drivers License			
☐ Other :	☐ Other :		Date Issued :	Expiration Date:

Witness Full name :	Phone number :
Email Address :	Witness Signature:
Address :	

Document Type	Date/Time Notarized	Document Type	Fee Charged
			Record Number

NOTES

NOTARY RECORD

Full name :	Phone number :	Thumb print :

Email Address :	Signature :
Address :	**Signer's Signature**

Service Performed	Identification		ID Number :	
☐ Jurat	☐ ID Card	☐ Credible Witness		
☐ Oath	☐ Passport	☐ Known Personally	Issued by :	
☐ Acknowledgement	☐ Drivers License			
☐ Other :	☐ Other :		Date Issued :	Expiration Date:

Witness Full name :	Phone number :
Email Address :	Witness Signature:
Address :	

Document Type	Date/Time Notarized	Document Type	Fee Charged
			Record Number

NOTARY RECORD

Full name :	Phone number :	Thumb print :

Email Address :	Signature :
Address :	**Signer's Signature**

Service Performed	Identification		ID Number :	
☐ Jurat	☐ ID Card	☐ Credible Witness		
☐ Oath	☐ Passport	☐ Known Personally	Issued by :	
☐ Acknowledgement	☐ Drivers License			
☐ Other :	☐ Other :		Date Issued :	Expiration Date:

Witness Full name :	Phone number :
Email Address :	Witness Signature:
Address :	

Document Type	Date/Time Notarized	Document Type	Fee Charged
			Record Number

NOTES

NOTARY RECORD

Full name :	Phone number :	Thumb print :
Email Address :	Signature :	
Address :	Signer's Signature	

Service Performed	Identification		ID Number :	
☐ Jurat	☐ ID Card	☐ Credible Witness		
☐ Oath	☐ Passport	☐ Known Personally	Issued by :	
☐ Acknowledgement	☐ Drivers License		Date Issued :	Expiration Date:
☐ Other :	☐ Other :			

Witness Full name :	Phone number :
Email Address :	Witness Signature:
Address :	

Document Type	Date/Time Notarized	Document Type	Fee Charged
			Record Number

NOTARY RECORD

Full name :	Phone number :	Thumb print :
Email Address :	Signature :	
Address :	Signer's Signature	

Service Performed	Identification		ID Number :	
☐ Jurat	☐ ID Card	☐ Credible Witness		
☐ Oath	☐ Passport	☐ Known Personally	Issued by :	
☐ Acknowledgement	☐ Drivers License		Date Issued :	Expiration Date:
☐ Other :	☐ Other :			

Witness Full name :	Phone number :
Email Address :	Witness Signature:
Address :	

Document Type	Date/Time Notarized	Document Type	Fee Charged
			Record Number

NOTES

NOTARY RECORD

Full name :	Phone number :	Thumb print :
Email Address :	Signature :	
Address :	**Signer's Signature**	

Service Performed	Identification		ID Number :
☐ Jurat	☐ ID Card	☐ Credible Witness	
☐ Oath	☐ Passport	☐ Known Personally	Issued by :
☐ Acknowledgement	☐ Drivers License		
☐ Other :	☐ Other :	Date Issued :	Expiration Date:

Witness Full name :	Phone number :
Email Address :	Witness Signature:
Address :	

Document Type	Date/Time Notarized	Document Type	Fee Charged
			Record Number

NOTARY RECORD

Full name :	Phone number :	Thumb print :
Email Address :	Signature :	
Address :	**Signer's Signature**	

Service Performed	Identification		ID Number :
☐ Jurat	☐ ID Card	☐ Credible Witness	
☐ Oath	☐ Passport	☐ Known Personally	Issued by :
☐ Acknowledgement	☐ Drivers License		
☐ Other :	☐ Other :	Date Issued :	Expiration Date:

Witness Full name :	Phone number :
Email Address :	Witness Signature:
Address :	

Document Type	Date/Time Notarized	Document Type	Fee Charged
			Record Number

NOTES

NOTARY RECORD

Full name :	Phone number :	Thumb print :

Email Address :	Signature :	
Address :	**Signer's Signature**	

Service Performed	Identification		ID Number :	
☐ Jurat	☐ ID Card	☐ Credible Witness		
☐ Oath	☐ Passport	☐ Known Personally	Issued by :	
☐ Acknowledgement	☐ Drivers License		Date Issued :	Expiration Date:
☐ Other :	☐ Other :			

Witness Full name :	Phone number :
Email Address :	Witness Signature:
Address :	

Document Type	Date/Time Notarized	Document Type	Fee Charged
			Record Number

NOTARY RECORD

Full name :	Phone number :	Thumb print :

Email Address :	Signature :	
Address :	**Signer's Signature**	

Service Performed	Identification		ID Number :	
☐ Jurat	☐ ID Card	☐ Credible Witness		
☐ Oath	☐ Passport	☐ Known Personally	Issued by :	
☐ Acknowledgement	☐ Drivers License		Date Issued :	Expiration Date
☐ Other :	☐ Other :			

Witness Full name :	Phone number :
Email Address :	Witness Signature:
Address :	

Document Type	Date/Time Notarized	Document Type	Fee Charged
			Record Number

NOTES

NOTARY RECORD

Full name :	Phone number :	Thumb print :
Email Address :	Signature :	
Address :	**Signer's Signature**	

Service Performed	Identification		ID Number :	
☐ Jurat	☐ ID Card	☐ Credible Witness		
☐ Oath	☐ Passport	☐ Known Personally	Issued by :	
☐ Acknowledgement	☐ Drivers License			
☐ Other :	☐ Other :		Date Issued :	Expiration Date:

Witness Full name :	Phone number :
Email Address :	Witness Signature:
Address :	

Document Type	Date/Time Notarized	Document Type	Fee Charged
			Record Number

NOTARY RECORD

Full name :	Phone number :	Thumb print :
Email Address :	Signature :	
Address :	**Signer's Signature**	

Service Performed	Identification		ID Number :	
☐ Jurat	☐ ID Card	☐ Credible Witness		
☐ Oath	☐ Passport	☐ Known Personally	Issued by :	
☐ Acknowledgement	☐ Drivers License			
☐ Other :	☐ Other :		Date Issued :	Expiration Date:

Witness Full name :	Phone number :
Email Address :	Witness Signature:
Address :	

Document Type	Date/Time Notarized	Document Type	Fee Charged
			Record Number

NOTES

NOTARY RECORD

Full name :	Phone number :	Thumb print :
Email Address :	Signature :	
Address :	Signer's Signature	

Service Performed	Identification		ID Number :	
☐ Jurat	☐ ID Card	☐ Credible Witness		
☐ Oath	☐ Passport	☐ Known Personally	Issued by :	
☐ Acknowledgement	☐ Drivers License		Date Issued :	Expiration Date:
☐ Other :	☐ Other :			

Witness Full name :	Phone number :
Email Address :	Witness Signature:
Address :	

Document Type	Date/Time Notarized	Document Type	Fee Charged
			Record Number

NOTARY RECORD

Full name :	Phone number :	Thumb print :
Email Address :	Signature :	
Address :	Signer's Signature	

Service Performed	Identification		ID Number :	
☐ Jurat	☐ ID Card	☐ Credible Witness		
☐ Oath	☐ Passport	☐ Known Personally	Issued by :	
☐ Acknowledgement	☐ Drivers License		Date Issued :	Expiration Date:
☐ Other :	☐ Other :			

Witness Full name :	Phone number :
Email Address :	Witness Signature:
Address :	

Document Type	Date/Time Notarized	Document Type	Fee Charged
			Record Number

NOTES

NOTARY RECORD

Full name :		Phone number :		Thumb print :
Email Address :		Signature :		
Address :		Signer's Signature		

Service Performed	Identification		ID Number :	
☐ Jurat	☐ ID Card	☐ Credible Witness		
☐ Oath	☐ Passport	☐ Known Personally	Issued by :	
☐ Acknowledgement	☐ Drivers License		Date Issued :	Expiration Date:
☐ Other :	☐ Other :			

Witness Full name :		Phone number :
Email Address :		Witness Signature:
Address :		

Document Type	Date/Time Notarized	Document Type	Fee Charged
			Record Number

NOTARY RECORD

Full name :		Phone number :		Thumb print :
Email Address :		Signature :		
Address :		Signer's Signature		

Service Performed	Identification		ID Number :	
☐ Jurat	☐ ID Card	☐ Credible Witness		
☐ Oath	☐ Passport	☐ Known Personally	Issued by :	
☐ Acknowledgement	☐ Drivers License		Date Issued :	Expiration Date:
☐ Other :	☐ Other :			

Witness Full name :		Phone number :
Email Address :		Witness Signature:
Address :		

Document Type	Date/Time Notarized	Document Type	Fee Charged
			Record Number

NOTES

NOTARY RECORD

Full name :	Phone number :	Thumb print :
Email Address :	Signature :	
Address :	Signer's Signature	

Service Performed	Identification		ID Number :	
☐ Jurat	☐ ID Card	☐ Credible Witness		
☐ Oath	☐ Passport	☐ Known Personally	Issued by :	
☐ Acknowledgement	☐ Drivers License			
☐ Other :	☐ Other :		Date Issued :	Expiration Date:

Witness Full name :	Phone number :
Email Address :	Witness Signature:
Address :	

Document Type	Date/Time Notarized	Document Type	Fee Charged
			Record Number

NOTARY RECORD

Full name :	Phone number :	Thumb print :
Email Address :	Signature :	
Address :	Signer's Signature	

Service Performed	Identification		ID Number :	
☐ Jurat	☐ ID Card	☐ Credible Witness		
☐ Oath	☐ Passport	☐ Known Personally	Issued by :	
☐ Acknowledgement	☐ Drivers License			
☐ Other :	☐ Other :		Date Issued :	Expiration Date:

Witness Full name :	Phone number :
Email Address :	Witness Signature:
Address :	

Document Type	Date/Time Notarized	Document Type	Fee Charged
			Record Number

Made in the USA
Monee, IL
13 August 2024

63809491R00056